Biographies of famous people
to support the curriculum.

Captain
Scott

by Emma Fischel
Illustrations by Dave McTaggart

W
FRANKLIN WATTS
LONDON•SYDNEY

First published in 1997
by Franklin Watts
This edition 2002

Franklin Watts
96 Leonard Street
London EC2A 4XD

Franklin Watts Australia
56 O'Riordan Street
Alexandria, Sydney
NSW 2015

© 1997 text Emma Fischel
© 1997 illustrations Dave McTaggart

ISBN 0 7496 4362 5 (pbk)

A CIP catalogue record for this book is
available from the British Library

Dewey Decimal Classification
Number: 910.91

10 9 8 7 6 5 4 3 2 1

Series Editor: Sarah Ridley
Designer: Kirstie Billingham
Consultant: Dr. Anne Millard

Printed in Great Britain

Captain Scott

When Robert Falcon Scott was born there were still lots of places in the world where few Europeans had been – except for a few brave explorers, that is.

One day baby Robert would grow up to become one of them.

Robert grew up in a big house by the sea with his four sisters and one brother. He longed to join the navy.

He was a bit of a daydreamer, though, and not very strong. Maybe the navy wouldn't want HIM.

"I know just the school to help Robert," said his father.

And it did help. At thirteen, Robert joined the navy.

For the next five years he trained hard on lots of different ships.

"He's just what we need," said his bosses in the navy. "He's keen, a good leader – and he works harder than anyone."

He never gives up!

Robert found some things easier
to learn than others.

And no one could teach him
how to stop being seasick.

When Robert was eighteen he met a very important man called Sir Clements Markham.

Sir Clements was planning a big expedition to study a faraway place called Antarctica.

He knew the expedition would take at least ten more years to prepare – and it would need a leader.

He already had his eye on Robert.

Sir Clements Markham

When Robert was twenty-five, the Scott family lost nearly all their money.

Robert sent home as much from his wages as he could. His brother in the army did the same.

It didn't leave them much.

Four years later his father died.

Then his brother caught a horrible disease called typhoid. He died too, aged twenty-nine.

At last something good
happened. Robert bumped into
Sir Clements Markham again.

"My expedition to study
Antarctica is ready to go!"
Sir Clements told him. "It will
be full of danger. Whoever goes
may never return!"

"I'd like to lead it!" said Robert. But some people thought a scientist should lead the expedition.

Sir Clements soon changed their minds.

Robert found out all he could about Antarctica.

Antarctica is a huge land covered in ice. It is the coldest and windiest place on earth. In winter the sun never rises, so it is dark day and night for months.

Hmmm. Rather a challenge.

NORTH POLE

ARCTIC CIRCLE

ANTARCTICA

SOUTH POLE

*F*ierce blizzards sweep across it. Huge cracks in the ice, hidden by snow and hundreds of feet deep, can swallow up men forever.

*T*he ice stretches miles out to sea. Only specially built strong ships can push their way through. Ordinary ships can be crushed to pieces.

Robert and his team travelled to Antarctica and studied it for two years. They got closer to the South Pole, the very bottom of the world, than anyone had before.

They found out important things about Antarctica and made maps of all the new places they went to.

When Robert arrived home, he was a hero! Everyone wanted to know about his time in Antarctica.

When he was forty he married
Kathleen Bruce, a sculptress.
But by now a plan was forming
in his head.

He would go back to Antarctica.
And this time he would try to
travel further than anyone had
yet been, all the way to the
South Pole!

News came of the first person to reach the North Pole.

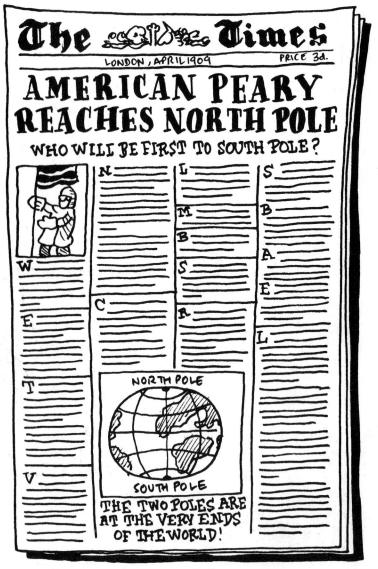

The Times

LONDON, APRIL 1909 — PRICE 3d.

AMERICAN PEARY REACHES NORTH POLE

WHO WILL BE FIRST TO SOUTH POLE?

NORTH POLE

SOUTH POLE

THE TWO POLES ARE AT THE VERY ENDS OF THE WORLD!

There was no time to waste!

"Britain shall be first to the South Pole," Robert announced. "My preparations are under way."

Then he announced something else.

Robert needed to raise lots of money. He travelled all over the country telling people about the expedition.

He organized every tiny detail
of the trip.

He even had special biscuits
baked that wouldn't freeze rock
hard in the Antarctic.

A year later Robert was ready. But so was someone else – a Norwegian explorer called Roald Amundsen.

The race was on!

It took six terrifying weeks to cross the stormy seas to the Antarctic.

The ship pushed its way through the frozen sea as close to the land as it could.

Then Robert and his team unloaded and dragged everything across the ice to the shore ...

or almost everything.

They built huts to live in. The huts were in ready-made sections which they had to fix together.

Inside the huts it was a bit of a squash.

The long, dark winter was on the way. They would have to wait for spring to start the long trek to the South Pole.

"We'll store food along the first part of the route right now," said Robert. "That will leave room for more on the sledges when we set off for the Pole."

Some of the men went off to look for fossils and rocks. But bad weather stopped them from getting back.

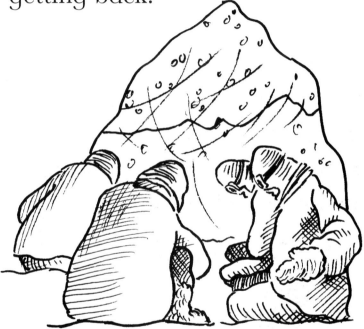

They made an ice cave and lived in it all winter. They ate seals and penguins and only just survived.

As spring approached, Robert began planning his route to the South Pole.

Meanwhile, further up the coast, Amundsen did the same.

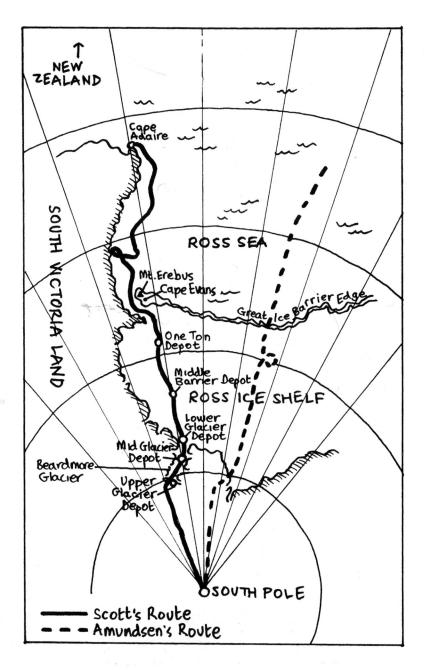

NEW ZEALAND

Cape Adaire

ROSS SEA

SOUTH VICTORIA LAND

Mt. Erebus
Cape Evans

Great Ice Barrier Edge

One Ton Depot

Middle Barrier Depot

ROSS ICE SHELF

Lower Glacier Depot

Mid Glacier Depot

Beardmore Glacier

Upper Glacier Depot

SOUTH POLE

——— Scott's Route
- - - Amundsen's Route

At last spring arrived. "We're off," said Robert – and so the journey to the South Pole began.

But soon a terrible blizzard struck.

Both the motorised sledges
broke down and, one by one,
the ponies collapsed. Pulling the
heavy sledges through the deep
snow was too hard for them.

Some ponies had to be shot.
They were buried in case they
were needed as food on the
way back.

The men had to climb a long,
steep river of ice, called a glacier.

The glacier was full of dangers.

It got rougher and steeper.
All the dogs were sent back and
the men had to drag the heavy
sledges themselves.

It took them nearly two months
to reach the top of the glacier.

Robert chose four men to go with him on the last part of the journey to the South Pole.

OATES SCOTT EVANS

BOWERS WILSON

For nearly two more weeks they struggled on. "Keep going," urged Robert. "Keep going!"

At last they reached the
South Pole.

But the Norwegians had beaten
them to it.

It had taken almost three months to get to the South Pole – longer than Robert had hoped. He knew the journey back would be much harder.

"Let's go," he said. "We can do it."

At first a strong wind helped them along. Then it turned against them.

The men struggled onwards, slower and slower. Snow began falling, harder and harder.

After a month of travelling, they were getting weaker by the day.

Evans fell and hurt his head badly. He never recovered.

"Courage," said Robert. "We HAVE to go on." But he wasn't sure how much longer they could.

The other men had made food stores, called depots, for them along the route back.

But they were going much slower now. Food from one depot was running out before they reached the next.

That made them even weaker – and even slower.

Another month went by.
Frostbite froze their skin and
made their fingers and toes
swell up. Captain Oates had it
worst. He could hardly walk.

One morning Oates opened the tent door. "I am just going outside and may be some time," he said quietly. Then he walked outside.

He never came back. He gave his life to try and save the others.

The worst blizzard of all swept down. The next depot wasn't far – but they just couldn't get to it. They waited in their tent. The food ran out. So did their fuel. They knew it was the end.

On the tenth day, they died.

Months later, a search party found their tent. They built a huge mound of snow over it and made a cross out of skis.

They found Robert's diary too.

Had we lived, I should have had a tale to tell of the hardihood, endurance and courage of my companions which would have stirred the heart of every Englishman. These rough notes and our dead bodies must tell the tale...

Further Facts

About Amundsen

Roald Amundsen had spent a lot of time in the Arctic, learning the best ways to survive extreme cold from the Inuit people who live there.

He started from sixty miles nearer the South Pole than Robert and moved much faster. All his team were good skiers, and they didn't have the heavy scientific equipment Robert had to slow them down.

He used no ponies, only fast husky dogs. He shot any exhausted dogs and fed them to the others.

About Antarctica

Antarctica is one of the few places in the world that has been hardly touched by humans.

Because Antarctica is so huge, any changes to it might change things everywhere. If more Antarctic ice melts, the sea levels and the weather might change also. In turn, that would affect us all.

So far, forty countries have agreed to protect Antarctica from any development for the next fifty years.

Some important dates
in Captain Scott's lifetime

1868 Robert Falcon Scott is born in Devon, England.

1880 Robert joins the navy as a cadet.

1900 Robert is invited to command the National Antarctic expedition.

1902 The National Antarctic expedition reaches Antarctica in January.

1904 Robert returns from Antarctica and is promoted to Captain in the navy.

1908 Robert marries Kathleen Bruce.

1909 Robert Peary reaches the North Pole.

1909 Robert's son, Peter, is born.

1910 Robert sets off for his second Antarctic trip.

1911 The journey to the South Pole begins on 1 November.

1911 Roald Amundsen reaches the South Pole on 14 December.

1911 Robert reaches the South Pole on 17 January.

1911 Petty Officer Evans dies on 17 February.

1911 Captain Oates walks out into a blizzard on 17 March.

1911 Robert writes his last diary entry on 29 March. He dies, aged forty-two.